Living with a
Silent Illness

Serenity Tipton

authorHOUSE®

AuthorHouse™
1663 Liberty Drive
Bloomington, IN 47403
www.authorhouse.com
Phone: 1 (800) 839-8640

Published by AuthorHouse 05/23/2017

ISBN: 978-1-5246-9231-5 (sc)
ISBN: 978-1-5246-9230-8 (e)

Library of Congress Control Number: 2017907986

Print information available on the last page.

This book is printed on acid-free paper.

Welcome to, "Living With A Silent Illness," A different look inside the world of Psychogenic Non-Epileptic Events, and how they affect the lives of hundreds of thousands of individuals. People from all around the world and from all lifestyles are living with this illness every day of their life. This book had been written with personal experiences, specialists, doctor's notes, along with other individual's opinions and testimonies, in addition to how they feel about living with Psychogenic Non-Epileptic Events (PNES) Non-Epileptic Seizures (NES). In this book, you will also find clinical research along with other information about Psychogenic Non-Epileptic Events, the silent illness.

TABLE OF CONTENTS

SEIZURE DISORDERS

Seizure disorders come in many forms and are often misdiagnosed. There are over 10 million people living with some type of event disorder, or seizure disorder, other than epilepsy. There are many types of seizure disorders, which do not have the same characteristics of a regular seizure since these types are more of a silent type of event. These types of events or attacks are also known as; psychogenic non-epileptic seizures (PNES), psychogenic non-epileptic events (PNEE), non-epileptic events (NEE), pseudo-seizures, and non-epileptic attacks (NEA). Many doctors and specialist are uncomfortable with explaining what NEE is or stands for, when giving a patient a conclusive diagnosis this can often confuse the patient and their families. With no certain diagnosis or taking a chance of being misdiagnosed, usually happen because there is not enough information out there for the doctors or specialist to tell their patients about their seizures or events they have been having. The patient knows something is not right and will continue to seek help elsewhere, only ending up with the same answers as before.

Many times the specialist and doctors just give you a diagnosis to satisfy your mind, and help you rest better. Nevertheless, not coming straight out and telling the patient the truth can cause more harm than good. Most neurologists will recommend you to see a psychiatrist, which in turn makes an individual think "is something wrong with me mentally," without that even being the case at all. Therefore, since the neurologist does not see anything physically wrong with an individual, he cannot give them a straight answer, many times leaving the patient more confused and concerned, to cause more anxiety for the patient.

According to Dr. Alsaadi and Dr. Marquez, from the University of California "all psychogenic non-epileptic seizures function as a coping mechanism. Patients with these events are more likely to use maladaptive coping strategies to handle stress. In psychogenic non-epileptic seizures, psychologic conflicts are translated into a physical symptom—the event/ seizure. Whereas, intolerable distress is dissociated from the painful conscious experience of the trauma or forbidden emotions that are causing the distress. Consequently, psychogenic non-epileptic events are not intentional: they are created as a psychologic defense mechanism to keep internal stressors out of conscious awareness" (Alsaadi T. & Marquez A., 2005). Everyone is born with his or her own coping mechanisms, and some cope more than others do when it comes to stressful situations. Nevertheless, some individuals coping mechanisms do them more harm, especially if they have had trauma, abuse, or some type of head injury.

Individuals with epilepsy and other seizure disorders tend to live ordinary productive lives, although their coping skills are not as good as their peers. Psychogenic non-epileptic events are a type of coping mechanism that tends to shut down the mind and body to defend its self from the distress it is under. Many NES patients are disabled and unable to live a productive happy life. Seizure disorders affect every age, race and gender, no one is excluded. In a group study of 10 individuals living with non-epileptic seizure or events, nine out of ten are disabled, while the other individual is in the process of becoming disabled. People living with Non-Epileptic Events have a limited lifestyle, and most usually has to be accompanied by another individual, which makes it hard to live a fulfilling life.

NON –EPILEPTIC EVENTS

Non-Epileptic Events are referred to as, physical symptoms of a psychological imbalance, and are involuntary movements, for the individual with PNEE. People store so much information and memories (good and bad) in their mind, although some memories are forgotten or hard to remember. Subconsciously those memories come back to the surface at times; with the happy memories, we rejoice in the good times, while others may not be so pleasant to remember. Hurley (2006) asks, "Have you ever heard of *stress causing seizures? Although you may not have, there are many cases of seizures being caused by stress.*" Learning relaxation techniques and methods of stress reduction helps to decrease the effects stress has on your body and your mind (Hurley T, 2006). While relaxation techniques may help some individuals, it is not a one size fits all. It would take many hours and a lot of money to find the underlying cause of why an individual has so much stress, and how to relieve that stress from their life.

As humans, we often block out the bad things that have happened to us in our lives, by blocking those terrible memories out of our minds, they can remain in our subconscious minds. So when diagnosed with Psychogenetic Non-Epileptic Events or Seizures, one does not always think of "*well now which one of those bad memories caused this?*" It is hard to find, diagnose, and pinpoint the exact point in time, or the events that had happened to bring you to this point, where you are now suffering the effect from PNEE, or having a seizure.

"One should be acquainted with a clinical presentation of PNES as well as its psychiatric origin in order to adequately recognize and treat the disorder" (Jain U, Jain J, Tiruveedhula V, Sharma A., 2013 (p.15 (6). Although one should be acquainted with clinical presentation of PNES, often which is hard to find, depending on your location, region, and how many doctors or neurologists are within that area, in which who are educated, and have the knowledge in the field of psychogenic non-epileptic seizures.

In the following paragraphs, Doctor Peter Pressman, MD (2016) will explain what Psychogenic Non-Epileptic Seizures (PNES) are, along with how the events or seizures can be treated.

Who Gets PNES? Psychogenic seizures may occur in any age group, but most commonly affects young adults. In addition, 70 percent of sufferers are <u>women</u>. There is frequently a psychiatric history and often a history of <u>abuse</u> or <u>sexual</u> trauma.

How are Psychogenic Seizures Treated? Education is critical, as learning about PNEE, and Conversion Disorders often affects how people recover. Educating yourself is empowering yourself

What Improves the Chances of Recovery From Psychogenic Seizures? People who are younger when the diagnosis is made, with few other complaints and milder episodes, have a higher chance of improving. The most important factor is the duration of the illness. If someone has spent years being treated for epilepsy, even if an individual has all the signs of a conversion disorder, that person is less likely to recover from psychogenic non-epileptic events/ seizures..

Like other forms of conversion disorder, PNES is a diagnosis of exclusion. This means that a doctor making this diagnosis should keep an open mind and consider the possibility that something besides a psychiatric complaint is causing the seizure activity, and then make every effort to rule out such possibilities. Similarly, it is important that patients keep an open mind about the possibility that their problem is psychological and get the help they need (Pressman P, (2016). Psychological factors play a big role when dealing with stress, and anxiety. When the body or brain is in distress, it can cause many psychological problems. Since the episodes do not show up on an EEG, they believe, it has to be psychological. Something in the brain is not functioning correctly and causes your body to just shut down due to an over load of stressors.

Non-Epileptic seizures are thought to be caused by many things. Through research and communicating with other PNEE and NES patients, here are some reasons that patients believe could be triggering their symptoms, along with other stress-related causes of PNEE include:

- ★ Head trauma
- ★ Physical abuse
- ★ Emotional trauma
- ★ Depression
- ★ Emotional abuse
- ★ Sexual abuse
- ★ Posttraumatic Stress Disorder
- ★ Anxiety disorders
- ★ Conversion disorder – the seizures themselves are the physical symptoms converted from the emotional distress.

Jain U, Jain J, Tiruveedhula V& Sharma A.(1013) believe that PNES is a somatic manifestation of mental distress, in response to a psychological conflict or other stressors (2013, p.15). While this statement may sound like "it is all in your head," this does not necessarily mean that it is all in your head, or that these symptoms are something that you have made up. Non-Epileptic Events/ Seizures are very real and should be taken seriously.

Any psychological stress exceeding an individual's coping capacity often produces psychogenic non-epileptic seizures (NES). Such as information overload and the, brain is not equipped to handle too many stressors at once. Receiving psychiatric treatment has been associated with a positive outcome in some studies but not in others" (Patient, Non-epileptic Seizures (n.d.). When an individual seeks psychiatric help for mental stress or anxiety issues, he or she is hoping for positive results, but as stated above, psychiatric help does not work for everyone.

EPILEPSY

Epilepsy is a type of seizure disorder. Nevertheless, with epilepsy, there is a problem in the brains electrical system causing neurons to misfire. A surge of electrical impulses which cause the brain to be altered, and cause a change in behavior, movement, feeling and awareness, which can last for several seconds to a few minutes. These types of seizures are epileptic seizures, but not all individuals who have seizures have epilepsy.

There are several different types of seizures, although the most well known type of seizure is epileptic. There are stress-induced seizures, diabetic seizures, epileptic seizures, psychogenic non-epileptic seizures, non-epileptic seizures, and the list can go on. With so many different types of seizure disorders, an individual can be diagnosed with more than one type of seizure disorder.

For many seizure disorders, there are still no known reasons why individuals have them. Some people are born with epilepsy, and some people get seizure disorders from head injuries. Seizure disorders very from different types of severity, along with the different type of seizure one may have, such as with epilepsy, it has to do with the brain, while psychogenic seizures and non-epileptic seizures, are psychological, and require mental health specialists.

Everyone is born with a seizure threshold. If your threshold is high, you are less likely to have a seizure. However certain activities or things, known as triggers, can lower your threshold, such as drinking alcohol, sleep deprivation, stress, illness, flickering lights and hormones (for women mostly) can have an impact on your seizure threshold (Swaner, 2012). A seizure threshold is the level of neurological stimulation capable of precipitating a seizure. The more relaxed, and healthy you are, the less likely you will have a seizure. A person does not have to have a seizure disorder to have an occasional seizure, as stated above; everyone is born with his or her own individual seizure threshold of just how much his or her body can take before it drops down into the seizure threshold. Knowing what your triggers are, can also help to prevent a seizure. Many healthy individuals have never had a seizure before, but this does not mean that they will not become ill with a high fever, and cause them to have a seizure. Although they may be healthy, the stress on an individual's body can produce a seizure.

TRIGGERS

"Psychogenic Non-Epileptic Seizures represents a chronic disorder with repeated triggering that could lead to a less significant role of the same psychological trigger" (Jain U, Jain J, Tiruveedhula V& Sharma A (2013, p.15). While doing thorough research, many people had some similar triggers, while others could identify most of their triggers that would cause them to have psychogenic non-epileptic seizure. Nevertheless, there are still so many individual that do not know, nor cannot pinpoint their triggers; the episodes just come on all at once.

There are many things and different situations along with feelings, which can trigger a psychogenic non-epileptic event. Not everyone has the same triggers, some maybe more sensitive to their triggers while others, have built up a tolerance level to which they have a trigger that causes them to have PNEE. Here are a few things that can cause triggers in an individual.

❖ Missed medication
❖ Lack of sleep
❖ Hormones
❖ Extreme emotional stress
❖ Low blood sugar
❖ Drugs or alcohol
❖ Flashing lights
❖ Mental distress
❖ Anxiety

In the wake of a seizure, it is often difficult to pinpoint the cause. After all, seizures are rather unpredictable and can be triggered by multiple, uncontrollable factors. However, if you can nail down a common factor, you may be able to avoid it and control the quantity and severity of your seizures (Fleet A., 2016). Emotional stressors are a primary source, of triggers, and cause seizures and events to happen. The seizures and triggers occur when an individual is under a large amount of worry, anger, and anxiety. The stressors, and anxiety, trigger something in your brain and body that cause them to shut down, or to cause a psychogenic non-epileptic event.

MENTAL DISTRESS

Mental distress; are you feeling mentally distressed? What are you feeling? Despite a complete physical workup and even a visit to a specialist or two, no one can find a reason behind your physical complaints; it may be that your body's way of letting you know that your mind is in distress. What does it mean by "your mind is in distress"? "Maybe you're having that "bad day" or perhaps a rough few weeks: Feeling down, anxious, overstressed, as if you're one breath away from the "last straw. "The presence of anxiety, or a depressive mood or of a conflict within the mind, does not stamp any individual as having a psychological problem, because, as a matter of fact, these qualities are indigenous to the species," says Charles Goodstein, MD, clinical professor of psychiatry at NYU Medical Center in New York City (Bouchez C. 2016). We know how life can get stressful at any given time; it is only natural to feel stress. So many individuals are so over come by stress that it interferes with their daily life. Therefore, too much stress on a person can actually cause them to have mental distress.

"Nevertheless, if living on the "last straw" has more or less become your way of life, experts say there is something on your mind that is crying out for your attention." Just because one seeks professional help through a psychiatrist or therapist, does not mean that something terrible is mentally wrong with them. Stress overload; if you are stressed most of the time and are irritable, for no apparent reason; you may be over stressed. Stress overload is dangerous to your physical and mental health. Seeking help is not a bad thing; it is called *taking care of you.*

ANXIETY / ANXIETY DISORDER

Anxiety and anxiety disorders are partially responsible, when it comes to psychogenic non-epileptic seizures. Many of these types of seizures or events can be caused by too much anxiety, or anxiety attacks. Although, many people may suffer from anxiety or an anxiety disorders, however, this does not by any means, to assume they will develop the illness of non-epileptic seizures. If you have anxiety problems, or reoccurring anxiety attacks, it is better to discuss them with your doctor.

Anxiety is something many people experience at some point in their lives, but for many anxieties becomes a way of life. Many people deal with anxiety in different ways; some people have some type of anxiety, when it comes to test, or getting a job done on time. Although many people have anxiety toward certain things there are so many people living with chronic anxiety disorders. There is a big difference when it comes to anxiety, and an anxiety attack or disorder.

Anxiety disorders are much different from the occasional anxiety one may feel from time to time. Anxiety disorders can cause distress on a person, which it interferes with their ability to lead a normal life. Individuals living with this type of disorder, can experience serious mental illness, worry and fear can become overwhelming for these individuals. However, there is help out there and the right type of medications can help reduce the anxiety, as well as, the anxiety attacks that come along with the anxiety disorder.

ABUSE

According to Neurology Now, "common psychological stressors include sexual or physical abuse, the death of a loved one, or distressing emotions that a patient needs to dissociate from. For some patients, the seizures are a manifestation of post-traumatic stress disorder. Many Psychogenic Non-Epileptic Seizures (PNES) patients have prior histories of psychological traumas or abuse. Psychogenic non-epileptic seizures are more common in young women, especially those who have had a history of abuse. Not all non-epileptic seizure patients have a history of physical or sexual abuse, and a head injury can contribute to non-epileptic seizures.

Non-Epileptic Seizures are NOT consciously produced by the individuals having the seizure; it is completely out of their control, that is why it is called the silent illness. In many cases seizures can be a result of high levels of stress, the seizure is the only way the body knows how to deal with the stresses of one's mind and body. Does being in an abusive relationship put pressure on your non-epileptic events? Yes, being in any type of bad relationship, or abusive relationship, can cause more mental distress, and cause episodes that are more frequent.

If an individual is often surrounded by negativity and abuse, or has a lack of support in their life, this could also produce more seizures. It is very important to get those types of people out of your life. Surround yourself with supportive, positive individuals, and people you can count on. It is going to take making changes in your own life, to help reduce the stress you are under and for the episodes to reduce.

There are so many people that have been abused or felt abused, at some point in their life. We as individuals need to stop the violence and abuse, to protect ourselves, and our families. Abuse can cause many mental health issues, and psychological problems, if not treated, or not treated in a timely manner. Do not beat yourself up for having Non-Epileptic Seizures (NES) or Psychogenic Non-Epileptic Events (PNEE), the fault is not your own, it is the abusers fault; it is never your own fault. No one deserves to be abused in any manner. An individual is not at fault or should they feel as though they had done something wrong to be over become by stress, and or mental distress, by the hands of the abuser. We are all individuals, and should be treated as such, with respect and dignity, do not let anyone take away your pride or lower your self –esteem.

In all the reading and research that has been compiled for the purpose of this book, this statement "sexual or physical abuse" has been used repeatedly. Therefore, one may ask them self, are rape victims, and abused woman, more acceptable to having psychiatric problems? Are abused children going to be troubled with Non-epileptic seizures? There are still so many questions and not enough answers, to this type if disorder.

Approximately 70% of Non-Epileptic Events (NEE) occur in women, and they can occur at different ages, but frequently begin in young adulthood (Seizure Smart, 2011). There are so many different names and diagnosis for these issues, which many doctors, neurologist, and psychiatrists find it hard to describe what exactly the diagnosis should be.

According to Tracy N. (2016), and other supporters, these are some symptoms that individuals have or had gone through, while dealing with their abuse.

Short-Term Effects of Emotional Abuse include:

- Anxiety or fear
- Shame or guilt
- Becoming overly passive or compliant
- Frequent crying
- Feeling powerless and defeated as nothing you do ever seems to be right

Long-Term Effects of Emotional Abuse:

- Depression
- Withdrawal
- Low self-esteem and self-worth
- Emotional instability
- Sleep disturbances
- Suicidal ideation, thoughts or attempts

WHAT IS SEXUAL VIOLENCE?

Sexual violence can be verbal, visual, or anything that forces a person to join in unwanted sexual contact or attentions. It can happen in different situations: in the home by someone, you know, a family member, on a date, or by a stranger. Although most sexual violence happens to young girls and women, it also happens to boys and men. Not all-sexual violence ends in rape, but if you are raped, you should seek help immediately.

Sexual violence and abuse or any type of sexual activity that you do not agree to:

- Inappropriate touching
- Vaginal, anal, or oral penetration
- Sexual intercourse that you say no to
- Rape
- Attempted rape
- Child molestation

These are important steps to take right away after an assault:

- Get away from the attacker and go to a safe place as fast as you can. Then call 911 or the police.
- Do not wash, or clean any part of your body. Do not change clothes, so the hospital staff can collect evidence.
- Go to your nearest hospital emergency room as soon as possible. You need to be screened for possible sexually transmitted infections (STIs) or pregnancy.

RAPE VICTIMS

In the United States, "More than 1 in 3 women (35.6%) and more than 1 in 4 men (28.5%) have experienced rape, physical violence, and/or stalking by an intimate partner in their lifetime", states a 2010 Summary Report of The National Intimate Partner and Sexual Violence Survey (Bhatti Shalu, (2014). According to The National Intimate Partner and Sexual Violence Survey: 2010 Summary Report, "Nearly 1 in 10 men in the United States has experienced rape, physical violence, and/or stalking by an intimate partner." A study by Appel & Holden, (1998); states that almost 30% to 60% of men who abuse their female partners also abuse their children in the house.

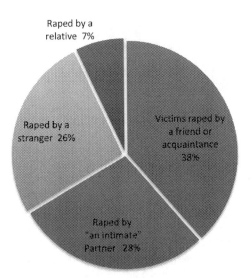

Abuse, rape, and sexual violence, are harmful to the human brain, and often cause an individual to have several mental issues, such as Post Traumatic Stress Disorder (PTSD). When an individual has gone through such a painful ordeal, it causes stress on the human brain, and causes psychological problems. The reason that these issues were brought out in this book is to inform others that NO type of abuse is healthy, for the person living with it, so it is always best to seek medical advice.

This book is not for those seeking medical reasoning, but to make one aware about Non-Epileptic Seizures (NES). NOT everyone who has survived a sexual assault, or rape, will be subjected to having any type of PTSD, or NES. Nevertheless, any type of rape or abuse will cause some type of emotional and mental health issues.

The information in this book is to make individuals aware of these disorders, and how to handle and deal with their own stressors in their life. Many violent attacks can leave a permanent smudge in ones brain, and when the brain feels overstressed by the emotions of this disorder, it shuts down ones body and mind, causing them to pass out, or to have a seizure. This is just one of many reasons why individuals are becoming ill with Psychogenic Non- Epileptic Seizures.

Sexual violence can happen at any age and to every, race, sex, and or religion. It can start out by a look or an unwanted touch; it can make a person very scared or nervous to be around that person. It is in families, with boyfriends or girlfriends, with friends, or even a family friend.

LIFE'S BAGGAGE

Everyone one in life is carrying around some type of baggage, everywhere they go their baggage goes along. Personal baggage from previous relationships, or other difficult times in one's life seem to come back to life in other relationships. For many the baggage tends to get heavier and heavier to bear on their own, from one stage of life to the next. So they may seek help to lighten the load, some individuals seek counseling, while others have support from family and friends. Many individuals baggage is often too hard to bear, or even to hard talk about with others. How big is your baggage of emotional pain that you carry along with you? Is it grief – anxiety – depression – shame – low confidence – betrayal – bad luck – or just sadness? Individuals need to know when to let go of all their excess baggage, and let someone else carry it for a while.

Sort out all your feelings, and determine what is important to you. Who is worth carrying heavy baggage for? Are you doing this to yourself, to drag yourself down because others want to make you feel bad? Do not let others determine what type of baggage you choose to carry with you through your life.

SERENITY'S EXPERIENCE

This is a version of how Serenity describes her psychogenic non-epileptic events / seizures. Serenity's Non-Epileptic Seizures (NES) affects her life in many ways. She cannot go on vacations alone; or go for long drives. Serenity states that she has to be very careful of what she does and is aware of her surroundings at all times. Serenity has social anxiety and depression, more now than before the seizures / events had started. Serenity often feels trapped and confined to her home, she use to love to do yard work and go fishing, and loved the outdoors, but since the events had started her life has dramatically changed, and in many ways stopped. Serenity becomes physically drained from mowing the lawn and working in the garden, that she has a blackout (Psychogenic Non Epileptic Event). Most times, she refers to her PNEE as blackouts or passing- out, because that is how it feels to her. There are so many activities that she loved to do, that are now limited, or some things that Serenity can no longer do.

In the last 16 years, Serenity feels as if she has become a prisoner to this silent illness, but she is fighting back and trying to get her life back. Although, she may not be able to do most things independently, she keeps trying; she will not let this illness get her down. The non-epileptic seizures are claimed to be brought on by mental and or physical stressors in her life. Serenity does not know the triggers that contribute to her episodes, so the reason she and other individuals that have these episodes or seizures on a daily basis are still unknown. Some doctors believe that non-epileptic seizures (NES) are physical reactions to emotional symptoms. Emotional symptoms can be from a wide range of thoughts and feelings that she feels throughout a day or period of time.

Serenity is just a young middle-aged woman in her mid 40's, although her PNEE had started when she was in her late 20's or early 30's. There was a lot going on in Serenity's life at that time, but nothing to serious to cause an illness like this to happen to her. Serenity was under quit a bit of stress at that time, and had a lot on her mind, maybe mental distress could have played a part in this diagnosis, but what ever it was, Serenity will never know.

In Serenity's young teenage life, she was sexually assaulted, and when she was in her 20's she had been raped, nevertheless she was in abusive relationships. Serenity had been abused physically, emotionally, mentally and sexually, but she would have never had thought that she would get an illness from her own pain and suffering. Serenity just could not understand of all the bad, painful, and wrong doings toward her, why was she the one still suffering, and the violators, still out there.

Through all of Serenity's research and reading different article about psychogenic non-epileptic events/ seizures, Serenity believes that she is a victim of posttraumatic stress disorder, but also an abuse survivor. Serenity hopes that with her voice and the voice of others, which they can all make PNEE / PNES a well-known name and for others to understand that the brain of an individual is very fragile. There are many different types of illnesses out there that can cause a persons brain to stop functioning like it should, one should always be aware of the different types of illnesses, such as the one's mentioned in this book. Psychogenic Non-Epileptic Events and Non-Epileptic Seizures are silent illnesses that affect thousands of individual's lives, and limiting there lives, such as in Serenity's story.

SERENITY'S EPISODES

According to an aeronautical engineer, Rully N." a rise in blood pressure or an increase in blood sugar may occur as a result of emotional strain due to excessive fear or to an accident involving severe emotional strain. The mere memory or association of some earlier incident later in life may provoke physiological reactions. *Continual worry* is one of the significant causes of physical reactions and symptoms leading to various physical disorders. Violent emotions or prolonged minor emotional disturbances can affect the mental activity and the function of certain body processes (Rully N., 2009)". Too much worrying and stressing over something you cannot control, can do quite a bit of damage to your mental and physical health.

Serenity was diagnosed with Non-Epileptic Seizures, and than Non-Epileptic Events 16 years ago, since then she has been on a personal mission to find the reason why she had fallen victim to this illness. The triggers for the episodes are unknown, although Serenity had kept journals of what happens before and after the episode, to help her better understand what brought on the event. Serenity had numerous tests and had seen multiple Doctors, Psychiatrists, Psychologists, Neurologists, and Counselors, as well as, Specialists and still no answers. There were several misdiagnoses before Serenity was diagnosed with Psychogenic Non-Epileptic Events (PNEE). Living with this silent illness has changed her life, and in many ways stopped life, as she had known it to be.

A typical episode (event), consist of a tired weak feeling, or sudden sleepiness, or too weak to move. Within seconds, Serenity would have to sit or lay down if possible as soon as she could feel the aura coming on. She would sit/lie there unable to move or respond, although she could hear what was going on around her, but Serenity cannot respond.

The episodes Serenity had experienced last anywhere from 20 minutes up to an hour, and occasionally up to two hours. When she would wake up or come out of an episode she would feel weak, unable to move, or movement was slow. Serenity states that she could not think clearly or focus; she seemed off balance, speech was stuttered, and slurred. According to Serenity it takes anywhere from 30 minutes to a few days to come all the way out of an episode and an aura before she can move around or talk normal again. She has had several times where the aura episode lasted a few hours to a few days before she was back to herself, and then it would happen again, Serenity has these non-epileptic seizures/ events everyday. This is just a vicious cycle, which she has tried hard to correct, and has done extensive research to help her after exhausted all other options.

<u>Symptoms that occur with Serenity's episodes before she passes out</u>

- ★ Confusion
- ★ Light headed
- ★ Weakness
- ★ Tired /Fatigue
- ★ Lose of muscle tone
- ★ Feeling faint
- ★ Yawning

Not all non-epileptic seizure patients have a history of abuse, just as not all non-epileptic seizure patients have a history of a head injury. Many patients have a history of sexual or physical abuse. While trying to narrow down the symptoms of non-epileptic seizures many patients had similar symptoms during their episodes, while others had different types of symptoms during their non-epileptic seizure episodes.

DOCTOR'S NOTES

Serenity had also offered the results from her recent hospital stay for monitored video EEG. The results; characterized by feeling dizzy, lightheaded followed by the body becoming limp and unresponsiveness were captured with no epileptiform EEG correlate consistence with Psychogenic Non-Epileptic Events. Interictal EEG was also normal with no epiletiform discharges (Yadala, S. M.D. 2016 (p.6, 12, 13).

1. Date of event: Sep. 26, 2016
    <u>Clinical Description</u>: Patient is lying in bed in a semi-reclined position. She activates the event button and closes her eyes. She remains in bed with her eyes closed for approximately 20 minutes. The patient later reported that she had a typical event and was thought that she was "unconscious" for about 30 minutes.
    <u>Electrographic Description</u>: There is no epileptiform EEG correlate to this event. Initially, there is a posterior dominant rhythm seen and then she drifts into drowsiness and early sleep.

2. Date of event: Sep. 27, 2016
    <u>Clinical Description</u>: After performing hyperventilation and photic stimulation, patient reports feeling lightheaded. She then breathes deeply. About 8 minutes later, she activates the event button. She activates the event button another time two minutes later. She then lays in bed with eyes closed and remains unresponsive to verbal, tactile, and noxious stimulation. Her pupils are normal size and reactive to light. She is occasionally seen blinking her eyes subtly. This event lasted approximately 20 minutes.

Electrographic Description: There is no epileptiform EEG correlate to this event. A normal background and posterior dominant rhythm are seen.

3. Date of event: Sep. 27, 2016
   Clinical Description: Patient is lying in bed. She then closes her eyes and lays in bed without obvious movement. The patient later reported to the staff that she was unresponsive.
   Electrographic Description: There is no epileptiform EEG correlate to this event. Initially, there is a posterior dominant rhythm seen and in 3 minutes, she drifts into N2 sleep.

4. Date of event: Sep. 27, 2016
   Clinical Description: The event begins after hyperventilation is performed. Initially she reported that she might pass out when the technician asked her to move the left arm, she said she could not. She then closed her eyes and became unresponsive with no response to painful stimulus. She was not responsive to verbal stimuli. There was no twitching noted. After about 7 minutes, she opens her eyes but is very sluggish to answer questions and states that it takes a couple minutes before she can recover completely.
   Electrographic Description: There is no epileptiform EEG correlate to this event. The EEG findings are similar to her usual background.
   The one channel EKG lead showed heart rate of approximately 80 bpm.
   Impression: This EEG demonstrates normal electroencephalographic patterns. The four typical events captured on this study described as "being unresponsive" by patient, without response to stimuli given by medical staff and/or with eyes closed had no epileptiform EEG correlate.
   Clinical Correlation: The four typical events captured on this study as described in detail above had no epileptiform EEG correlate and are consistent with Psychogenic Non-Epileptic events.

Psychogenic seizures or events are caused by subconscious thoughts, emotions, or stress not abnormal electrical activity in the brain. Through research and reading different types of material, they all have a symptom in common such as stressors, emotional, and physical. While looking at Serenity's doctors notes about her Video EEG, Serenity seems to be relaxed, and just laying in bed watching the television with out any physical stressors going on. Serenity seems to be relaxed, so that would cancel out the emotional stressors, unless she had been thinking of different things that would cause her to become mental or emotional distressed in order for her to have a PNEE. Either way, an individual does not always necessarily have to be under a certain amount of stress, or distress to have a psychogenic non-epileptic event / seizure.

Psychogenic non-epileptic events are in the same category as the psychogenic non-epileptic seizures. "Psychogenic non-epileptic seizures (PNES) are events that resemble epileptic seizures, but occur without epileptiform activity and instead stem from a psychological source "(Myers L, Fleming M, Lancman M, Perrine K, 2013). This meaning that there is nothing to see on an EEG because they are non-epileptic. Epileptic seizures will show up on an EEG since it has to do with misfiring of certain neutrons in the brain.

Psychogenic non-epileptic events are a type of coping mechanism that tends to shut your mind and body off to defend its self from the distress it has been over loaded with. After many years of hopelessness, and tons of research, there is still no answers to all the questions, people have about PNEE/ NES. In Serenity's quest to find out what it is that is, actually causing her events is still a mystery, for herself and the team of doctors she has been seeing. Psychogenic Non-Epileptic Seizures (PNES) are not noticeable to the average person, but it is very serious for the individuals living with this illness.

STRESS

It had been said for years, even decades that stress, is the main leading cause of many illnesses and ailments. Everyone one has experienced stress, at some point in their life, if you have not yet experienced it, it wont be too long before stress creeps into your life. Stress can create seizures, and other mental health issues. An individual needs to be able to handle and cope with the stress in their lives, if one is unable to handle the stress or respond in a proper way, the stress can continue to manifest into a seizure, as well as, mental health issues.

Stress affects most people in some way. Stress leads to rapid changes within the entire body, the heart, blood vessels, immune system, lungs, digestive system, brain, and sensory organs. Stress plays an important role is responses to danger, and ones coping mechanism. Stress is not always a bad thing it is beneficial to individuals, and is often harmful is one stays in a stressful state for long or continuous amounts of time. Bad stress can lead to chronic problems both physical and psychological, causing several types of illnesses, and other ailments to the body, and the brain such as having a seizure. Stress induced seizures, are a manifestation of psychogenic non-epileptic seizures, or events.

TESTIMONIALS

The following are personal stories from individuals living with non-epileptic seizures or psychogenic non-epileptic events. Many individuals may have recently been diagnosed, while so many others have been fighting for years for answers to the causes of Non-Epileptic Seizures (NES) and Psychogenic Non-Epileptic Events (PNEE).

Tami (*Feb. 2012*):

> I have been told that the triggers for my seizure are: heat, light, exertion, noise, sounds, and mental stress. How do you treat those? I am just upset that I cannot do things with the family (11 and 8 year-olds in the house). They want to go swimming, but I am not able to go. They want to go to a water park, but I am not able go. Do I try to hold them back? No! I feel too guilty. I am tired of it all.
>
> *Serenity also has triggers for her events on occasion, such as loud sounds, anxiety, and mental distress. Serenity had first started having these events while her children were between the ages of 10 and 13 years of age. Yes, it really does put a damper on your life and family events.*

Leon (*Feb. 2012*):

> My triggers are interactive TV, flashing lights, to much computer time, physical exercise, even taking a shower will trigger an attack or walking more than a few yards, too much going on around me, fed up with theses darn seizures ruling my life. I would also like to add that

most seizures have no triggers the worst wake me in the night with full violent convulsions and that, stress does not play a part at all in my seizures.

(May 2017)

Recently I have started having B12 injections every other day on a long-term basis. With having B12 Deficiency treated, these injections will hopefully go some way to help repair the nervous system. I am already showing small but definite signs of repair to neurological symptoms in some areas. They may or may not eventually help with the seizures.

The real bad trigger I have found is very common with non epileptic seizure sufferers as well as those who have epilepsy is CFS lights which we come into contact with florescent lights that are everywhere, including hospitals, and shops. I cannot bear the strong florescent lights, even when wearing dark glasses for more than 10 minutes, or I get a buzzing/ flickering feeling in my head, followed by a seizure.

I have also found that this is common for autistic children also and there is a thought that Functional Neurological Disorder (FND) has a connection with the autistic spectrum as well.

Serenity is not always aware of what her triggers are, just a few, but the other episodes just come on for no apparent reason at all. Serenity does not recall having any issues with the florescent lights in hospitals, although she can not drive at night due to the headlights on cars, especially the florescent ones. Serenity has the deepest sentiment for you, and she can relate when you stated, "you were fed up with theses darn seizures ruling my life" Serenity feels the same way.

Shannon (*July 2008*):

> I have had a seizure disorder for 21 years and finally in
> April 2010, I was diagnosed with Psychogenic Non-
> Epileptic Seizures PNES. Living with this illness is
> depressing and hard, but the only thing I can do is keep
> telling myself it's ok, and keep your head up. You are
> not crazy and unfortunately, there is nothing you can
> do about this.

> *When Serenity first started having her events/ seizures
> she had thought she was going crazy as well, she did not know
> what to do or what was going on with her. Life had gotten her
> down and she has gone through depression and so many life-
> changing events. As Shannon had stated, "there is nothing
> you can do about this" it seems as if, once an individual starts
> having bad seizures, the more likely it is for them to continue
> to have a seizure disorder.*

These individuals have shared with us how their events or seizures
affect them and their personal lives. These individuals tend to have
the same type of misery and frustration in common "seizures." Some
individuals can feel when he/ she are going to have a seizure, while
others described what their triggers are. Many individuals know what
their triggers are, and how to avoid a seizure from coming on, although
there are some individuals that do not know theirs triggers or the cause
of them.

WHAT'S IN A NAME

In 2015, a study was performed of different individuals to determine the type of seizures or episodes they were having. Some of the results in this study need to be interpreted with caution. If not further specified, the term "non-epileptic seizure(s)," "non-epileptic attack(s)," "non-epileptic episode(s)," or "non-epileptic event(s)" may not entirely describe the psychogenic nature of the paroxysmal episode nor any underlying etiologic factors (Brigo, Igwe, Ausserer, Nardone, Tezzon, Giuseppe, Bongiovanni, Tinazzi, & Trinka. 2015, (p.21). Just hearing these diagnoses from a neurologist, or doctor, can make you panic, and have many more questions. So we have to ask ourselves what is in a name, and why so many names for something with so many common symptoms. The answer to that is still yet to be found.

Patients need to feel reassured and understand just what is wrong with them, or why they keep having these events or seizures. Many patients leave the neurologists office or their psychiatrist's office with just as many questions as when they have arrived. Feeling confused, and unsure of what is going on in their minds, and their bodies leaving them confused, and occasionally causing their anxiety levels to rise. "The apparent lack of interest by mental health professionals goes in parallel with the lack of training to manage psychogenic symptoms among neurologists.

Neurologists and epileptologists should be very well aware of PNES to make the correct diagnosis, to avoid unnecessary, inefficacious, and sometimes harmful antiepileptic treatment, and to plan the most appropriate management" The unavoidable consequence is that "patients will continue to find themselves caught between neurology and psychiatry" (Brigo, Igwe, Ausserer, Nardone, Tezzon, Giuseppe, Bongiovanni, Tinazzi, & Trinka. 2015, (p.24).

Psychogenic non-epileptic events or seizures is not something that is new to neurologist, or other specialist in this field, it has been around for decades. Nonetheless, no one seems to be able to give a correct diagnosis, or make help available to those living with this illness. Many doctors will just pass you on to a counselor, or psychiatrist for mental help. Why is it that so many individuals are living with PNEE /PNES and there is not more help or information that the specialist can give a person to better understand. Without knowledge, and understanding, many feel as if they have some type of mental problem, causing them to keep passing out.

Many individuals often wonder if psychogenic non-epileptic event / seizures are a type of mental illness. However, the events and seizures are brought on by mental distress, lack of coping mechanisms, and stressors in an individual's life. The episodes that individuals are having, come from the brain and the body, however; what about an individual's mental status. A conversion disorder is a type of mental illness, and many people with psychogenic non-epileptic events / seizures have also been diagnosed with a conversion disorder. Individuals are starting to question, are Psychogenic Non-Epileptic Events a mental disorder, or a mental illness? With the lack of information from doctors and specialist the answer is not know, since there is not enough information out there about PNEE, PNES.

MENTAL ILLNESS

There are more than 200 forms of mental illness. Some of the more common disorders are depression, bipolar disorder, dementia, anxiety disorders and panic attack disorder. With many individuals, living with some type of mental illness, some of there problems may be related to excessive stress due to a particular situation or series of events. Mental illnesses are often physical as well as emotional and psychological. Mental illnesses could be caused by environmental stresses, chemical imbalances in the brain, along with mental stressors of every day life.

Here are some signs of mental illness, but one also has to keep in mind that not all mental illness are seen. Psychogenic non-epileptic events and non-epileptic seizures are a type of silent illness, but does it really fall under the mental illness category? More research is still needed to determine if it is in fact a mental illness.

Signs of mental illness:

- Confused thinking
- Prolonged depression (sadness or irritability)
- Feelings of extreme highs and lows
- Excessive fears, worries and anxieties
- Social withdrawal
- Strong feelings of anger
- Growing inability to cope with daily problems and activities
- Suicidal thoughts
- Numerous unexplained physical ailments

Mental illness can be painful, and make ones life miserable. The stigma, and the way the world views individuals with mental illness can be cruel. An individual cannot help it if they have a mental illness; all he or she can do is seek help to control the illness. For many individuals living with a silent illness they often have reoccurring and prolonged depression, or become manic-depressive. There is counseling, and medications that can help those individuals, nevertheless; with taking the prescribed medications and seeing a counselor on a regular basis many individuals still suffer from depression.

With mental illness causing so many issues, and leading to other illnesses such as psychogenic non-epileptic events / seizures, and non-epileptic seizures, one is bound to start feeling the effects of this silent illness in their every-day life. Like so many individuals living with a mental illness, psychogenic non-epileptic seizures patients can also feel much of the same signs and symptoms. Individuals' living with PNEE experience social withdraws, because they are afraid of having a seizure or an event out in public or in unfamiliar surroundings. This fear can carry over to excessive fear, and anxiety, which can make individuals more likely to isolate themselves to feel safe.

There are so many cases where an individual with non-epileptic seizures / events, and those living with a mental illness have thought about, attempted, or even succeeded at committing suicide. The stress, anxiety, and life's pressures become too much and cause individuals to take their own life. This is something that needs a closer look and these individuals need to be monitored so that they do not attempt suicide. Individuals living with a mental illness are more prone to having other unexplained physical illnesses as well.

FIND THE ANSWER TO YOUR QUESTIONS

The information below is used as an educational aid only. It is NOT intended as medical advice for individual conditions or treatments. Talk to your doctor, neurologist, therapist, psychiatrist, or consult with your pharmacist before following any medical regimen to determine what is safe and effective for you. This book is based on personal experiences, along with other resources that were personally used in this research for answers to this illness. If you believe that you or a loved one may have any of these symptoms or believe they may have some type of seizure disorder, please contact your doctor.

Explaining seizures that are not epileptic:

http://www.epilepsysociety.org.uk/AboutEpilepsy/Associatedconditions/Non-epilepticseizures

Non-epileptic Seizures:

http://www.drugs.com/cg/non-epileptic-seizures.html

Nonepileptic Seizures (NES) - Topic Overview

http://www.webmd.com/epilepsy/tc/nonepileptic-seizures-nes-topic-overview

What are non-epileptic seizures:

http://my.clevelandclinic.org/ccf/media/Files/Epilepsy_Center/08_NEU_060_NonEpilepsyPatient_v2.pdf

DEFINITIONS

The following are definitions to words; some individuals may not understand what these words really mean. Here is a break down of some of the words used in this book.

Aura - Unusual sensations or movements that warn of an impending, more severe seizure. These auras are actually simple focal seizures in which the person maintains consciousness.

Cataplexy - A sudden loss of muscle tone that leads to feelings of weakness and a loss of voluntary muscle control. The most severe attacks result in a complete loss of tone in all voluntary muscles, leading to total physical collapse during which individuals are unable to move, speak, or keep their eyes open.

Convulsions - Sudden contractions of the muscles that may be caused by seizures.

Conversion Disorder - Conversion disorder, also called functional neurological symptom disorder, is a condition in which you show psychological stress in physical ways.

DSM – Stands for the Diagnostic and Statistical Manual of Mental Disorders

Epilepsy - A brain disorder in which clusters of nerve cells, or neurons, in the brain sometimes signal abnormally.

Epileptiform - Resembling epilepsy or its manifestations.

Mental Illness - is a disease that causes mild to severe disturbances in thought and/or behavior, resulting in an inability to cope with life's ordinary demands and routines.

Narcolepsy - Is a chronic disorder of the central nervous system characterized by the brain's inability to control sleep-wake cycles. People with narcolepsy experience irresistible and sudden bouts of sleep, which can last from a few seconds to several minutes.

Non-Epileptic Seizures (NES) - Are often mistaken for epileptic seizures, but are not caused by neurological disorders.

Non-Epileptic Events (NEE) - Also know as psychogenic non-epileptic seizures, are sudden, involuntary changes in behavior, sensation, motor activity, (including a change in the level of consciousness) or blood pressure, heart rate linked to psychological or social distress.

Pseudo-seizures - A physical manifestation of an emotional disturbance. They resemble epileptic seizures.

Psychogenic - Means beginning in the mind.

Psychogenic Non-Epileptic Seizure - (PNES) - Attacks that may look like epileptic seizures, but are not caused by abnormal brain electrical discharges. They are a manifestation of psychological distress.

Somatic - Pertaining to characteristics of the body

Somatization Disorder - Is a long-term (chronic) condition in which a person has physical symptoms that involve more than one part of the body, but no physical cause can be found.

REFERENCES

Alsaadi T. M.D. & Marquez A. M.D., 2005 _Psychogenic Nonepileptic Seizures_

Bhatti Shalu, (2014) Buzzle, Abusive-_relationship-statistics_.

   http://www.buzzle.com/articles/abusive-relationship-statistics. html#top

Bouchez C. (2016), _Experts describe the physical and mental signs that may indicate emotional distress._ Emotional Distress, 10 Signs of an Ailing Mind

   http://www.webmd.com/mental-health/ features/10-signs-ailing-mind

Brigo F., Igwe S., Ausserer H., Nardone R., Tezzon F., Giuseppe L., Bongiovanni, Tinazzi M., & Trinka E. _Terminology of psychogenic nonepileptic seizures._

Epilepsia, 56(3):e21–e25, 2015 doi: 10.1111/epi.12911

   http://eds.b.ebscohost.com.proxy-library.ashford.edu/eds/pdfviewer/ pdfviewer?vid=1&sid=74ef4d04-e95a-4371-b2df-725d1103759 f%40sessionmgr102&hid=126

Fleet A, (2016), _7 Common Seizure Triggers_

   http://www.activebeat.co/your-health/women/7-common-seizure-triggers/?utm_medium=cpc&utm_source=bing&utm

campaign=AB_BNG_US_DESK&utm_content=search&utm _term=non%20epileptic%20seizures

Healthwise 2015, Nonepileptic Seizures (NES) - *Topic Overview.* WebMD.

http://www.webmd.com/epilepsy/tc/nonepileptic-seizures-nes-topic-overview

Hurley T, 2006 *Stress Causing Seizures*

http://stress.lovetoknow.com/Stress_Causing_Seizures

Jain U, Jain J, Tiruveedhula V, Sharma A. (2013) *Psychogenic non-epileptic seizures.*

Myers L, Fleming M, Lancman M, Perrine K, (2013) *Stress coping strategies in patients with psychogenic non-epileptic seizures and how they relate to trauma symptoms, alexithymia, anger and mood.*

http://ac.els-cdn.com.proxy-library.ashford.edu/ S1059131113001313/1-s2.0-S1059131113001313-main. pdf?_tid=4a3c62be-c2da-11e6-adb6-00000aacb360&acdnat= 1481815528_c51e2dad8e5f6dea8341d9686bf4f392

National Institute of Neurological Disorders and Stroke, 2011 *Narcolepsy Fact Sheet*

http://www.ninds.nih.gov/disorders/narcolepsy/ detail_narcolepsy.htm

Patient, (n.d.) Non-*epileptic Seizures*

http://patient.info/doctor/non-epileptic-seizures

Pressman P, MD, (2016) *Psychogenic Nonepileptic Seizures Explained,* Updated September 02, 2016

https://www.verywell.com/psychogenic-nonepileptic
-seizures-2488847

Prim Care Companion CNS Disord. p.15 (6)

https://www.ncbi.nlm.nih.gov/pubmed/15227961

Rully N, 2009 *Symptoms of Emotion*

http://ezinearticles.com/?Symptoms-of-Emotion&id=3240523

S.A.F.E. Inc.

http://safeshelter.net/s-a-f-e-inc/what-is-sexual-assault/

Seizure Smart, (2011) *Epilepsy Action Australia*

https://www.epilepsy.org.au/sites/default/files/Seizure%20
Smart%20-%20Non-Epileptic%20Events.pdf

Stump E, (2008) Neurology Now: *The Seizures No One Wants to Talk About* Volume 4(6); p 23-26

http://www.aan.com/elibrary/neurologynow/?event=home.
showArticle&id=ovid.com%3A%2Fbib%2Fovftdb%
2F01222928-200804060-00016

Swaner N. (2012) *15 Fascinating Facts About Epilepsy*

http://listverse.com/2012/04/30/15-fascination-facts-about-
epilepsy/

Tracy N. (2016) Effects *of Emotional Abuse on Adults*

http://www.healthyplace.com/abuse/emotional-psychological-
abuse/effects-of-emotional-abuse-on-adults/

University of California, Davis, Medical Center, Sacramento, California *Am Fam Physician*. 1;72 (5):849–856. http://www.aafp.org/afp/2005/0901/p849.html

Yadala, S, M.D. 2016 (p.6, 12, 13) *Medical report*

http://itgsuperstarwallpaper.blogspot.com/2012/10/dizziness.html

Serenity Tipton, <u>Living With Non-Epileptic Seizures</u> Synopsis Page
Serenity Tipton

701 Cedar St.
Poplar Bluff, Mo. 63901
1-573-840-5018

There are hundreds of thousands of individuals living with Non-Epileptic Seizures (NES) and Psychogenic Non-Epileptic Events (PNEE) all around the world. This powerful, packed book explains in detail what all of the medical terms are, along with important information for individuals living with NES – PNEE. The information in this book is for both the individual living with this illness as well, as their caregivers.

This book does not have chapters, but it does have sections, such as Seizures Disorder, Mental Distress, Abuse, Personal Stories, along with Testimonials of other individuals I had talked to. This is not a "one size fits all" type of book. There are so many different names and diagnosis for these issues, which many doctors, neurologist, and psychiatrists find it hard to describe what exactly the diagnosis should be. With anticipation by reading this book, it will help individuals and their families to better understand what Psychogenic Non-Epileptic Seizures, and Non-Epileptic Events.

Who Gets PNES? Psychogenic seizures may occur in any age group, but most commonly affects young adults. In addition, 70 percent of sufferers are women. There is frequently a psychiatric history and often a history of abuse or sexual trauma. How is Psychogenic Seizures Treated? Education is critical, as learning about PNEE, and Conversion Disorders often affects how people recover. Educating yourself is empowering yourself.

Printed in the United States
By Bookmasters